INTERIOR
details

25 fabulous finishing touches

INTERIOR
details

25 fabulous finishing touches

ANDREA SPENCER

PHOTOGRAPHY BY GRAHAM RAE

LORENZ BOOKS
NEW YORK · LONDON · SYDNEY · BATH

This edition published in 1996 by Lorenz Books
an imprint of Anness Publishing Limited
administrative office: 27 West 20th Street
New York, NY 10011

© 1996 Anness Publishing Limited

Lorenz Books are available for bulk purchase for sales
promotion and for premium use. For details write or call
the manager of special sales, Lorenz Books,
New York, NY, 10011; (212) 807-6739

ISBN 1 85967 219 1

Publisher: Joanna Lorenz
Senior Editor: Lindsay Porter
Photographer: Graham Rae
Designer: Lilian Lindblom
Stylist: Andrea Spencer

Printed in Singapore by Star Standard Industries Pte Ltd.

CONTENTS

INTRODUCTION

Trimmings can completely change the look and personality of everyday objects, such as lampshades and bases, simple tablecloths and fine muslin curtains. They need not be expensive and many can be created using everyday things from around the home. Search cabinets and drawers for balls of string and lengths of twine. Don't just wrap packages in corrugated paper – create beautiful surrounds for windows or doors and cover notebooks, candles and even straight-sided vases with it.

Take beautiful objects from nature to adorn your walls and windows. Make use of shells, pebbles and driftwood brought home from beachcombing vacations by fashioning them into pretty necklaces, glorious seaside curtains and unusual frames. Tiny flower heads, seeds, berries and leaves can all be used as decoration; when giving presents, make the occasion really special by wrapping them in delicate organza and tying them with a glorious bow. Ribbons can be used to dress windows, tie up napkins or adorn lampshades for the most beautiful light show ever. It's just a matter of having the confidence and style to get to work and start creating.

As with so many things, simplicity is key. Take a fresh look at a skein of raffia: it could look marvelous edging shelves or tied into a tassel to hold a napkin. Likewise, a few lengths of rope can be used to dress up your sofa, trim your curtains or create a dado in the bedroom or bathroom. Where possible, use natural materials, such as cotton, linen and burlap; they have a wonderful tactile quality and look good in any situation.

Experiment a little and gain inspiration from the ideas and projects on the following pages.

ROUND-UP WITH RIBBONS

Ribbons come in a wonderful variety of colors, textures and widths. By tying a simple loop or bow, you can give a new contrasting or complementary accent to existing furniture and accessories. Soft, floppy, translucent organza ribbons create a frothy cloud when gathered in folds and bows but look simple and elegant hung against the light of a window, where they lend an element of privacy and shield the eye from an unwelcome view without blocking the light at all. Rich silken ribbons, or rough linen and burlap, have completely different qualities.

Above: Often the simplest of materials are the most beautiful. Scrolls of handmade paper tied with ribbon are elegantly minimalist.

Above: Translucent ribbons used as a curtain, trimmed with dried flower heads.

Above: Dressing a lampshade with a simple organza bow, as here, creates an elegant effect. Try different ribbons to suit the style of the room.

Left: Organza ribbon on a twig and ivy wreath not only embellishes the decoration but is also used for hanging.

TASSELS

Tassels are flourishes: they bring a jaunty, nonchalant air to whatever they embellish. Tassels come in a wide variety of materials and colors. The simplest can be homemade from household materials such as string, which is perfectly in keeping with decorated old terra-cotta pots. Made from natural materials, they bring a touch of style to design schemes based on neutral colors and natural fabrics; in rich colors and silken threads they can be opulent or restrained, depending on how they are combined. Rich red combined with a natural linen table napkin is a sunburst of bright color that brightens but doesn't disrupt the neutral scheme. A traditional white tassel combined with a brick-red throw quilted in a simple, modern style is a graphic and contemporary interpretation of a classic upholstery trimming.

Above: The simplicity of the plain muslin curtain and bamboo poles has been complemented by the natural tassel. The effect is understated yet eye-catching.

Above: Decorated plant pots are enhanced by a homemade string tassel.

Above: Brightly colored tassels make the simplest and most chic napkin rings. Choose colors that complement your china: they could be matching or vividly contrasting.

Left: An upholstery tassel gives a sophisticated finish to the corner of a throw.

IN THE CARDS

Homemade cards go beyond mere stationery, and can become miniature works of art in their own right. Use to grace a mantelpiece or occasional table. You can start with store-bought plain blank cards or search for wonderful textured paper and cardboard to make your own. Then collect pressed leaves, flower heads and other natural materials, and combine these with contemporary details such as gold paint and ink and organza ribbon. For a perfectly simple, contemporary interpretation, take the plainest white card and embellish it with a graceful paper curl – minimalism at its best.

Above: A contemporary white card simply adorned with an orange paper curl creates a striking effect.

Right: This plain gold card is beautifully decorated with an oak leaf and ribbon.

Opposite: Decorating plain handmade paper with natural materials produces true works of art.

TURNING THE CORNER

The corners and edges of throw pillows are a good place for embellishments, especially when, as shown here, the covering fabric is plain. These details maintain and enhance the style of the pillows, which are made from natural materials in a range of neutral colors, as are the trimmings themselves. This example shows how you can make detailed decorations with traditional sewing and embroidery techniques but interpret them in contemporary materials. The result is fully in keeping with today's fashion for interior-design schemes based on natural materials.

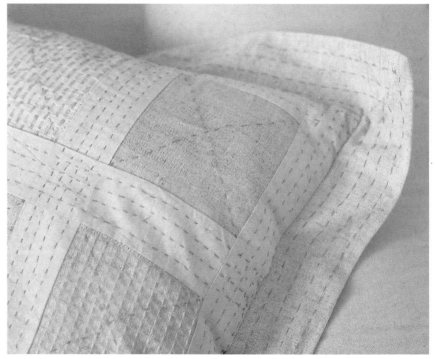

Above: White cords are simply sewn to an off-white, rough linen cushion, with graceful loops at the corners.

Above: Running-stitch "quilting" creates a neutral-on-neutral interpretation for a cushion.

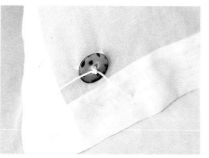

Left: A "tortoiseshell" button and string trim on snowy-white linen provides an elegant finish using the simplest of materials and techniques.

Above: Edge a cushion with toning beads on natural twine. Contrasting buttons can be used as accents of color, picking up the shades in the rest of the decor.

STICKS AND STONES

Treasures from nature are the perfect embellishments for decoration schemes based on natural fabrics and colors. Needing no craft or art to give them charm, natural objects have their own intrinsic beauty of form, texture and color. You may well have souvenirs of beachcombing, mountain walks, strolls though autumnal woods or spring fields that you would like to preserve; once you have the idea, every trip outdoors becomes a potential treasure-hunting expedition, if you just keep your eyes and your mind open. Collections of shells, stones, leaves and driftwood can be assembled as decorative focal points that can be rearranged or reassembled elsewhere in a moment. Alternatively, give your treasures a more permanent home by incorporating them into furnishings and accessories.

Above: A shell collection on a window ledge makes a beautiful display, with translucent shells glowing when the sun shines through them.

Right: Shells can be used as candleholders if you make sure the bases are stable.

Above: This vase is adorned with colored stones and pieces of glass worn smooth by the action of the waves. Use as many or as few as you wish to create the finish you desire.

Right: Wicker slippers are adorned with the tiniest of starfish.

SHELL-SHOCKED

Wandering along the seashore collecting shells is a wonderfully relaxing pastime. Rather than simply heaping your finds on the windowsill, turn them into something special. We have used lengths of fine voile for curtains and added interest to the top with eyelets and string loops.

To continue the theme, a really easy, yet effective, way of trimming a wall is to use a length of fine rope (available from craft or boating supply stores). Attach this to the wall at dado height; it would also be effective at picture-rail height. Attach a row of tiny shells above it. To complete the light, airy feel, paint an old terra-cotta pot white and attach a small sand dollar or other shell to the front.

YOU WILL NEED

- ♦ iron-on interfacing (if required)
- ♦ tape measure
- ♦ dressmaker's scissors
- ♦ cotton voile, the required drop, and 4 x the window width
- ♦ dressmaker's pins
- ♦ needle and basting thread
- ♦ sewing machine
- ♦ matching sewing thread
- ♦ chrome eyelets
- ♦ hammer
- ♦ wooden block
- ♦ rough natural string
- ♦ glue gun and glue sticks
- ♦ electric drill, with very fine drill bit (optional)
- ♦ fine beading wire
- ♦ beading needle (optional)
- ♦ terra-cotta pot
- ♦ matte white latex paint
- ♦ paintbrush
- ♦ sand dollar

1 To give extra body to the headings of fine fabrics, cut a length of iron-on interfacing 2 in wide and bond it to the wrong side of the voile.

2 Pin, baste, press and machine-stitch the heading across the top and the hem at the bottom. Then turn under a ½-in hem down each side, pin, baste, press and sew.

3 Mark the positions of the eyelets with pins.

5 Cut equal lengths of string to tie through the eyelets.

7 Cut lengths of wire and use a glue gun to stick them onto the shells.

4 Attach the eyelets following the manufacturer's instructions. Find a secure surface, such as a wooden block, before hammering the eyelets in place. One short, sharp blow with the hammer should do the trick.

6 Thread the strings through the eyelets and knot the ends.

8 Alternatively, drill holes in the shells. You might find a combination of these methods helpful, depending on the shape of the shells.

9 Postition the shells on the curtains.

11 Paint the flowerpot white.

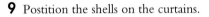

10 "Sew" the shells onto the curtain by hand, as invisibly as possible, with the beading wire.

12 Put a little glue on the side of the pot and attach the sand dollar.

Top and above: Even as light filters through the muslin, the wire fixings in the shells remain invisible.

Opposite: Voile curtains are threaded on a bamboo pole, which is in keeping with the natural feel of the decoration. Part of the charm is that the pole is slightly crooked.

LEADING LIGHTS

Lighten up! Change your shade and lamp base within the space of an hour to something quite sensational. Here, a basic shade was decorated with rough string threaded through punched holes. It is very easy to punch holes around the top and base of any shade, using a hole punch, and then thread through raffia, ribbon or yarn. To continue this idea, put small string bows at intervals around the shade and intersperse them with dried leaves.

YOU WILL NEED

♦ lamp base and shade

♦ hole punch

♦ rough string

♦ scissors

♦ glue gun and glue sticks

♦ dried leaves

1 Punch evenly spaced holes around the top and bottom of the shade. Oversew lengths of string through the holes, top and bottom.

2 Use the glue gun to stick the leaves around the shade.

3 Tie small string bows and glue them between the leaves.

4 Put a line of glue down the back of the lamp base. Starting from the top, bind a long length of string tightly around the stem. Use a second piece of string to cover the base. Press to secure the binding. Make sure that the ends are firmly in place.

LIFE'S LITTLE LUXURIES

Throw pillows are the perfect way to add a certain style to your room, as well as an element of comfort. Here, the natural tones and fabrics perfectly complement the simplicity of the sofa. Interest was added to the restrained look with decorative ties, looped buttons and a simple rope trim. If you want a change from the neutral color scheme shown here, add vibrant splashes with blues, reds, oranges and purples. On another note, blue and white always looks fresh and pretty.

YOU WILL NEED

ROPE-TRIMMED PILLOW

- ♦ about 2 yd fine-gauge rope
- ♦ dressmaker's pins
- ♦ plain linen pillow cover
- ♦ needle and matching thread
- ♦ pillow insert

PILLOW WITH TIES

- ♦ pillow insert
- ♦ tape measure
- ♦ cotton duck
- ♦ dressmaker's scissors
- ♦ dressmaker's pins
- ♦ needle and basting thread
- ♦ sewing machine and matching thread

LOOP AND BUTTON PILLOW

- ♦ pillow insert
- ♦ linen
- ♦ dressmaker's scissors
- ♦ dressmaker's pins
- ♦ needle and basting thread
- ♦ sewing machine and matching sewing thread
- ♦ iron
- ♦ 8–10 small buttons

1 For the rope-trimmed pillow cover, use the fine-gauge rope to experiment with different designs. When you are happy with the result, pin the rope to the cover.

2 Hand-stitch the cord to the cover, neatly finishing off the ends. Slip in the pillow insert.

3 For the pillow with ties, measure the pillow insert and cut one piece of fabric the depth of the pillow plus ⅝ in all around for seams. Cut another piece to twice the length, plus an extra 6½ in for the turning (this allows ⅝ in for a hem also). Pin, baste, press and sew, taking in the seam allowance.

4 Trim and zigzag stitch the raw edges together, to neaten them. Turn the pillow right-side out.

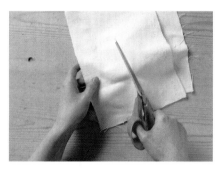

5 For the ties, cut six pieces of fabric measuring 2¼ x 11 in.

6 Fold each piece in half lengthwise with wrong sides together and pin, baste, press and machine-stitch a ½ in hem around two sides. Clip the seams and corners. Turn the ties right side out and slip-stitch the ends closed.

7 Position the ties in pairs and pin and baste them in place. Then top-stitch them securely in position.

8 For the cushion with loops and buttons, measure the width and length of the pillow insert. Double the length and add 4 in for the flap opening, plus 1¼ in for seams all around. You will also need to cut a 3-in wide strip the depth of the pillow plus seams. Cut fabric to this size and fold it in half.

9 To make the piping for the button loops cut a length of fabric about 1 in wide, on the bias. With wrong sides together, pin, baste and machine-stitch the fabric. Trim close to the stitching and, using a small safety pin, turn the fabric through to the right side. Press flat.

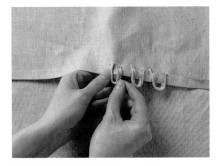

10 Measure the buttons and cut the loops to the correct size. Turn over the seam allowance on the cover, then pin and baste the loops in place.

11 Pin, baste and sew the interfacing strip for the back opening on the edge with the loops.

12 With right sides together, sew a seam all around the pillow. Turn right-side out and press. Mark the positions of the buttons with pins, and sew in place.

Right: These throw pillows complement the simplicity of the decor. Interest is added with flamboyant ties and other trimmings.

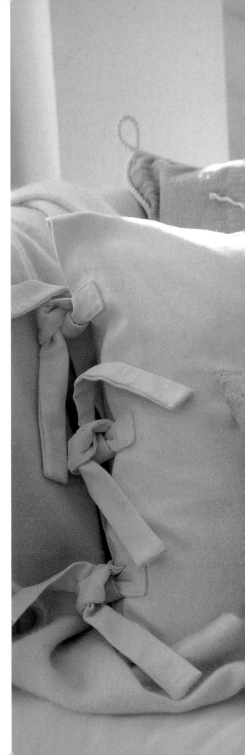

IT'S A WRAP

When decorating a table for a very special occasion, go to town and trim accordingly. These ideas could not be simpler to achieve but will add to the festive spirit.

YOU WILL NEED

- ♦ teapot
- ♦ scissors
- ♦ about 4 in square organza, net or other fine fabric
- ♦ potpourri
- ♦ very fine string
- ♦ small cinnamon stick
- ♦ glue gun and glue sticks
- ♦ glass bottle
- ♦ star anises
- ♦ decanter
- ♦ organza ribbon
- ♦ heart-shaped silver bead
- ♦ fresh rose
- ♦ painted jar
- ♦ florist's wire
- ♦ small fresh flower sprigs

1 For the teapot decoration, cut a circle from the organza square. Fill it with potpourri. Tie the top with string. Twist a cinnamon stick into the tie. To finish, tie the bag to the knob of the teapot.

2 To make the bottle necklace, cut a piece of fine string, and pull apart to separate the strands. Glue star anises to one strand. Knot the ends and hang it on the bottle.

3 To decorate the decanter, thread the heart-shaped bead onto a piece of organza ribbon. Knot it around the neck of the decanter and tie in a fresh rose head.

4 To decorate the painted jar, tie a very fine string around the neck. Wire together two or three strands of flowers and secure under the string. Tie an organza bow around the knob of the lid.

THE NEW WAVE

Corrugated paper is an often-overlooked material that can be absolutely stunning if used innovatively. It is easy to work with and has myriad uses. Experiment with different shapes to see which looks most pleasing. Triangles would look great bordering a door frame, for example, and perhaps following the lines of the skirting. Bear in mind that corrugated paper crushes very easily so, before starting work, flatten it with a ruler. It will still look ridged but won't become dented. A lovely idea is to paint corrugated paper white and then slit the corrugations, for a two-tone effect. Colored corrugated paper is available from art supply stores.

YOU WILL NEED

- tape measure
- roll of natural corrugated paper
- scissors
- ruler
- thin cardboard
- pencil
- craft knife
- self-healing cutting mat
- aerosol adhesive
- masking tape (optional)
- candles
- white latex paint
- paintbrush
- glue gun and glue sticks
- natural string
- straight-sided vase
- fine corrugated paper in different colors
- paper glue

1 Measure the width of the sill and cut the corrugated paper to this measurement, plus the required drop. Flatten the ridges with a ruler.

2 Draw the design onto cardboard and cut out to use as a template.

3 Draw the shape on the natural corrugated paper, using the template. Cut it out with a craft knife on a cutting mat.

5 For the candle-wrappers, cut strips of corrugated paper to the right size and paint them with white latex. Slit the corrugations with scissors.

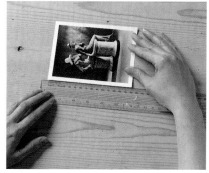

7 To make the picture frame, measure the image that is to be framed and decide on the size and shape required.

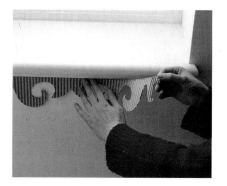

4 Spray the back of the paper with adhesive and fix in position. If you want to remove it later, stick masking tape under the windowsill and glue the decoration to the tape. You can peel off the tape without harming the wall.

6 Cut out a wider strip and glue it to the back of the white strip. Wrap it around the candles. Cut enough string to wrap several times around the candles. Use the same technique to decorate a straight-sided vase.

8 Draw the frame backing onto corrugated cardboard and cut it out with the craft knife and ruler.

9 Use the backing as a template to trace and cut out the front of the frame from colored corrugated paper. Cut out the central frame area.

11 Make a stand for the frame, with a piece of corrugated cardboard cut to the shape shown. Decorate the frame with twisted strips of colored paper.

10 Stick the image in position with paper glue so the backing color shows through in a thin border all around.

Right: Use corrugated cardboard and paper to make borders for windows and doors. Complete the look with candleholders, picture frames and book covers.

HANGING AROUND

Make the prettiest of chandelier-hangings with simple twigs such as apple or pear branches. Select a few branches and bind them together to make a pleasing shape, then hang the decoration in the center of a window, from a ceiling rose in a hallway or as a wall decoration. Trim the branches with crystal droplets, tiny pearls, and other little decorations, all fixed with the finest gold twine.

YOU WILL NEED

♦ 2 to 3 apple or pear tree branches

♦ fine gold wire

♦ scissors

♦ 1 yd gold cord

♦ crystal droplets

♦ gold beading wire

♦ small pearls

♦ gilded decorations

1 Take the branches and move them around until they form a pretty shape. Bind the branches together at the top with fine gold wire.

2 Attach a length of gold cord to hang the branches

3 Thread crystal droplets onto gold wire. Make short strings of pearls. If you like, combine some of the pearls with crystals.

4 Wire the remaining decorations, then twist the wires to make hanging loops. Position the twig chandelier, and then hang on the jewels.

SEASIDE SETTING

Soothe the soul by strolling along the seashore and at the same time, scour the beach for wonderful finds: strands of seaweed, pieces of driftwood, soft gray pebbles, feathers and chalky white stones with holes ready-made for threading onto pieces of twine. Make the most of your natural resources by using them to beautify mirrors and picture frames, or any other plain objects. Seashells make wonderfully evocative candleholders, and can be used as a central part of the table setting for a sea-themed dinner or party.

YOU WILL NEED

DRIFTWOOD AND PEBBLE FRAMES
- ◆ distressed-wood frames
- ◆ white glue (optional)
- ◆ medium-grade sandpaper
- ◆ wood stain and paintbrush (optional)
- ◆ about 20 in thick rope
- ◆ staple gun or hammer and tacks
- ◆ driftwood
- ◆ glue gun and glue sticks
- ◆ seaweed
- ◆ pebbles and stones
- ◆ seashells

PEBBLE AND STONE NECKLACES
- ◆ raffia
- ◆ tiny pebbles
- ◆ colored sea glass
- ◆ glue gun and glue sticks

SHELL CANDLEHOLDERS
- ◆ burnt-down candles
- ◆ kitchen knife
- ◆ seashells
- ◆ safety matches

1 For the driftwood frame, first check that the frame is sturdy and re-glue the joints, if necessary.

2 Sand the frame along the grain and stain it, if you like.

3 To hang the mirror, attach the rope to the top of the frame, using a staple gun or hammer and tacks.

5 Use a glue gun to fix the driftwood in place, making sure the pieces are perfectly secure.

7 When you are happy with your design, glue the pebbles and other materials in place.

4 Arrange your pieces of driftwood around the frame. Experiment with different positions until you are happy with the result.

6 Position the seaweed so it drapes gently across the mirror. Then add the pebbles, stones and seashells, raising them slightly off the edge so they are reflected into the mirror.

8 For the pebble frame, use a base similar to the driftwood frame's and sand and stain as before, if required. Select a pleasing variety of stones and arrange and glue them onto the frame.

9 For the pebble and stone necklace, tie a length of raffia around tiny stones and pieces of smooth colored glass.

11 For the candles in shells, cut the candles down with a knife and stand them in a shell. Light the candles and let the wax drip until it fills the shell. Blow out the flame. The wax then hardens in the shape of the shell.

10 Use a glue gun to apply a tiny dot of glue to each knot where the stone or glass is tied.

Right: This delightful seashore-themed arrangement evokes the pleasure of beachcombing in all seasons.

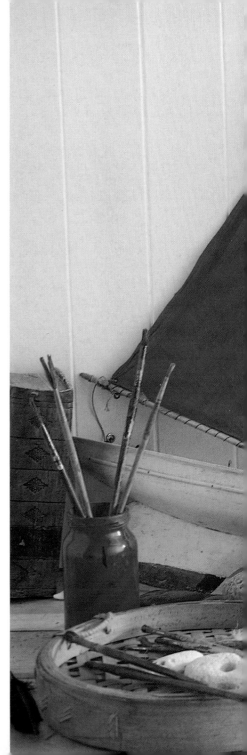

SELF-CONTAINED

There is a variety of boxes available, ranging from simple white wooden boxes to shoe boxes. Make a set of three using natural materials. Boxes can be trimmed with anything: bottle tops, paper clips, string, rope or a collage of stamps. Linen tape is available from notions departments.

YOU WILL NEED

♦ plain wooden box
♦ tape measure
♦ scissors
♦ linen tape
♦ needle and matching sewing thread
♦ 2 wooden beads or toggles
♦ glue gun and glue sticks
♦ larch twig
♦ small slatted wooden box
♦ small packet of potpourri
♦ small Shaker-style box
♦ dried leaves and pinecones

1 Measure the plain wooden box. Allow an extra ¾ in at one end for the toggle and about 3 in for the loop and tag. Cut two lengths of linen tape to this length. Sew a loop in the end of each tape and attach the beads to be used as toggles.

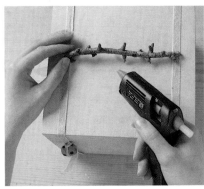

2 Secure the tape to one end of the box with glue, leaving the toggle and loop free so the lid can be opened. Repeat on the other side. Glue a larch twig to the top of the lid, as a decorative "handle."

3 For the slatted wooden box, sort through the potpourri and choose the items you would like to use. Glue them to the lid. Glue the dried leaves and pinecones to the Shaker box, and glue linen tape around the sides.

4 Tap
work
of wri

5 Tap
see the

Crea

snou

cris

impi

ti

f

fr

used

you l

Th

furnit

lette

and

10 For the monogrammed hand towel, use paper cutouts to plan your design.

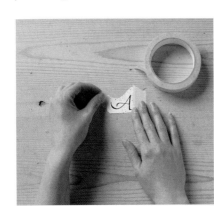

11 Tape the chosen letter flat on to a work surface.

12 Lay the towel over the alphabet, and tape flat.

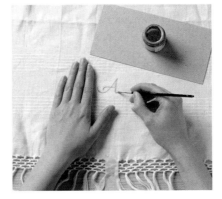

13 Trace over the letter onto the towel with fabric paint.

14 If you wish to apply an initial to a chair or other piece of furniture, put carbon paper on the back of the photocopied lettering, or rub all over the back with a soft pencil. Then transfer this to the chair by going over the outline with a harder pencil. Paint over the outline and leave to dry.

Opposite: Gold calligraphy on the sheerest of materials adds elegance to a corner of a room. Look out for mottoes or phrases appropriate to the location.

NEW WAYS WITH NAPKINS

Napkins in jewel-bright colors add a wonderful splash of brilliance to any table and immediately conjure up visions of hotter climes and exotic places. Choose yarns in strong colors to edge the napkins and trim each one in a different style, adding buttons and beads where appropriate.

YOU WILL NEED

- ♦ colored linen napkins
- ♦ colored tapestry yarns
- ♦ tapestry needle
- ♦ large button
- ♦ about 50 tiny multicolored beads
- ♦ tailor's chalk (optional)

1 If your napkin has an openwork edging, work cross-stitch following the decorative holes in the edge. If not, work evenly spaced cross-stitch along the edge. Attach a button with tapestry yarn at one corner.

2 Work the edge of a second napkin with blanket stitch (see Techniques). To make the tie, take a few strands of yarn, knot them in the center and stitch them to one corner.

3 For the bead edging, work out a design by arranging the beads on a flat surface. You could mark these on the napkin first, by chalking tiny dots where you want the beads to be. Sew the beads securely in place.

4 Complete the edging with running stitch. Simply take the thread and weave it in and out of the fabric at regular intervals, to form a pretty line of stitches about ½in from the edge.

SPARKLY GLASS

The plainest glasses and decanters can look extra-special when dressed with delicate strands of gold, diamanté and jewel-colored stones. For a party when you want to create a splash for one evening, these can be temporary arrangements, using masking tape sprayed gold and arranged in different patterns. The tape can be peeled or washed off after use. If you are prepared to spend a little more time, paint the glasses and glue stones on for good.

YOU WILL NEED

- ♦ masking tape
- ♦ self-healing cutting mat or cardboard
- ♦ gold aerosol paint
- ♦ scalpel
- ♦ metal ruler
- ♦ various glasses
- ♦ flat-backed diamanté jewels
- ♦ glue gun and glue sticks or other adhesive
- ♦ burnt match
- ♦ tweezers
- ♦ gold or silver beading wire
- ♦ decorative beads
- ♦ dried leaves
- ♦ gold ribbon

2 Spray the tape with gold aerosol paint, and leave to dry.

3 Using the scalpel and metal ruler, cut the tape into fine lengths about ¼ in wide.

1 Lay strips of masking tape across the cutting mat or cardboard.

4 Apply the strips to the bowls of the glasses, keeping clear of the rim.

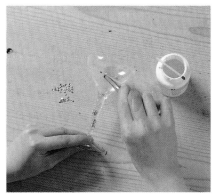

6 Stick the jewels directly to the glass, positioning them with a pair of tweezers.

8 Thread a decorative bead onto the wire halfway up the stem. Secure with a dab of glue.

5 To stick diamanté jewels to the glasses, use a glue gun and glue sticks, or use a burnt match to apply small spots of your chosen adhesive.

7 Attach beading wire by winding a long length around the top of a glass. Crisscross the wire down the glass.

9 Alternatively, twine wire around the stem, wrapping it several times quite loosely.

11 Again, thread a decorative bead on to the wire halfway up the stem. You can create all kinds of variations on this theme for a set of glasses.

12 Dress the stems of glasses with leaves, sprayed gold or silver. Attach them by slotting them into a ribbon around the stem of the glass.

Right: Turn plain glasses into festive and opulent vessels with gold and diamanté jewel decorations for a truly baroque-style special occasion. The effect can be created temporarily or permanently.

CURTAIN CALL

This is a quick and effective way to trim the top edge of a looped curtain. Tie ribbons around the loops and hang a selection of beautiful decorations from them. Here we have used pieces of potpourri, but you could also use odd earrings, bells, tin stars, buttons and so on. If you have a pinch-pleated or a simple gathered curtain heading, a small bow or knot with ribbon hanging down would look nice.

YOU WILL NEED
- ♦ tape measure
- ♦ ½ in wide burlap or linen ribbon or tape
- ♦ dressmaker's scissors
- ♦ needle and matching sewing thread (optional)
- ♦ potpourri
- ♦ glue gun and glue sticks

1 Decide the length of ribbon needed in relation to the drop of the curtain, so that it looks proportional.

2 Cut the ribbon to length, angling the ends so they look neat. If you are using a ribbon that frays, hem the ends. Select the pieces of potpourri that most complement one another.

3 Using a glue gun, attach the pieces of potpourri to the ends of the ribbon.

4 Tie the ribbon to the curtain loops. It is better not to attach the ribbon permanently, so you can change the design when you wish and take it off when you wash the curtains.

LOVELY LINENS

Pretty up plain linens with splashes of vibrant color. To add definition, run strips of rickrack around; for frilliness, buy a length of eyelet lace and sew it to the pillowcase. You could weave tapestry yarn through the eyelet lace in place of ribbon, to add color. Alternatively, look for linens that have a fine-holed edging and thread them with fine tapestry yarn. To complement the edges, add tiny crosses of colored thread to buttons sewn on the pillowcase. A more time-consuming but very eye-catching decoration is made by scalloping the edge of a sheet.

YOU WILL NEED

- ◆ paper
- ◆ pencil
- ◆ cardboard
- ◆ scissors
- ◆ single or double white sheet
- ◆ sewing machine
- ◆ white sewing thread
- ◆ small, sharp-pointed scissors
- ◆ red tapestry yarn
- ◆ tapestry needle
- ◆ plain pillowcase
- ◆ 3 yd eyelet lace
- ◆ dressmaker's pins
- ◆ needle and basting thread
- ◆ buttoned pillowcase, with fine-holed decorative edge
- ◆ glue gun and glue sticks
- ◆ decorative red buttons
- ◆ small pillow, with frilled-edge and center-opening cover

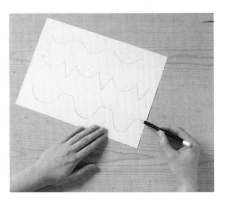

1 Try various design options for the shape of the scalloped edge of the sheet, or trace the pattern from the back of the book, enlarging if required.

2 Transfer your chosen design to cardboard and cut out the pattern for the sheet edging.

3 Put the pattern on the edge of the sheet and draw around it all along the edge. Use machine satin-stitch to go over the outline, using the closest stitch possible. Very carefully cut along the sewing line, close to the sewing but taking care not to snip any stitches. Cut lengths of tapestry yarn and knot the ends.

4 Sew the lengths of tapestry yarn through the sheet, leaving the long ends to form a decorative edge.

5 Edge the plain pillowcase with eyelet lace, pinning and basting it in place. Machine-stitch it securely.

6 Using a tapestry needle, thread the tapestry yarn through the holes in the eyelet lace.

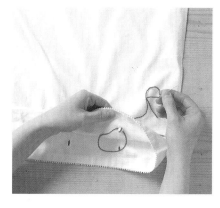

7 For the buttoned pillowcase, make neat cross-stitches over the buttons with tapestry yarn.

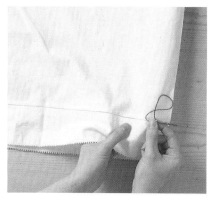

8 Thread tapestry yarn through the fine-holed decorative edge.

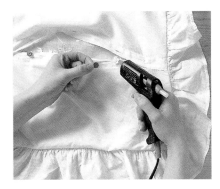

9 Use a glue gun to apply decorative red buttons to existing buttons on the frilled-edged cushion cover.

Right: A whole variety of ideas for bed linen and cushions is shown here, all using a red and white theme that would be perfect for warming up a neutral color scheme.

FABULOUS FURNITURE

Trim a perfectly plain sofa with a strand of rope that curves gently down the edge of the arm and across the base. This works extremely well in a white-on-white scheme, because the eye is aware of the shape but the embellishment doesn't jump out. Other types of trimming for sofas could be raffia edging, linen tassels or fringe.

YOU WILL NEED

♦ graph or plain paper

♦ pencil

♦ rope the length of the area you wish to trim

♦ clear adhesive tape

♦ scissors

♦ dressmaker's pins

♦ needle and strong sewing thread

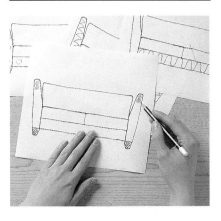

1 Work out different designs for the rope on paper, to see what works best; this style seemed sympathetic to the shape of the arm of the sofa and the lines of the seat.

2 Bind clear adhesive tape around the ends of the rope, so that the ends don't fray once the rope is in position.

3 Cut as close to the end of the tape as you can, so that as little is left as possible, but it still holds the rope firmly. Pin the rope onto the sofa and hand-stitch in place.

UNDER COVER

A seat cover in a yellow check is a lovely way to trim a chair and hide an ugly seat. Chair covers bring instant color and style to a room; using yellow checks and stripes immediately brings to mind buttercups, marigolds and the countryside. A pretty frill around the edge finishes off this seat cover, giving the chair great femininity and charm.

YOU WILL NEED

- ♦ tape measure
- ♦ paper, for template
- ♦ pencil
- ♦ scissors
- ♦ fabric (see step 1 to calculate the amount)
- ♦ dressmaker's scissors
- ♦ piping cord
- ♦ needle and basting thread
- ♦ sewing machine with zipper foot
- ♦ matching sewing thread
- ♦ iron
- ♦ about 1 yd tape

1 Make a paper template of the chair seat. Use the template as a guide to cut out the fabric with a ⅜ in seam allowance all around. For the frill, cut a piece twice the circumference of the seat with a 4-in drop, plus a ⅜-in seam allowance all around.

2 Cut a length of piping cord and a 1 in strip of fabric the length of the four sides of the chair seat. Fold the fabric around the piping cord, with wrong sides together. Pin, baste and stitch.

3 Hem the frill. Sew a line of running stitches around the top of the frill and then gather it up evenly.

4 Sandwich the piping cord between the frill and the seat cover, right sides together. The piping and frill will extend around the front and sides of the seat cover. Pin, baste, press and machine-stitch all around, clipping the corners so the frill sits properly. Attach lengths of tape to the back of the seat cover, to tie the cover in position.

CREAM TOPPING

Make a grand statement at the window by creating a pelmet with a curved edge trimmed with rope. The gentle wave of the pelmet gives a very gracious, elegant appearance to the treatment, which could, if you wish, be echoed in the edging of a loose cover on a chair or sofa. Another wonderful idea is to continue the pelmet around the room, so it acts as a wavy trim to the whole area. In this instance, make sure the pelmet is the same color as the ceiling so it doesn't interrupt the eye's progress. Pelmets can be any shape or size; experiment with pointed V's with bells on, castellations and the like. Cut the shape out of paper first and pin it above the curtains to see how it will affect the room as a whole.

YOU WILL NEED

- ◆ tape measure
- ◆ paper, for template
- ◆ 2 plates
- ◆ pencil
- ◆ pelmet fabric
- ◆ dressmaker's scissors
- ◆ interfacing
- ◆ dressmaker's pins
- ◆ needle and basting thread
- ◆ sewing machine
- ◆ matching sewing thread
- ◆ iron
- ◆ rope
- ◆ wooden batten
- ◆ hammer and tacks or Velcro

2 Cut two pieces of fabric for the back and the front of the pelmet. Cut out interfacing to stiffen the pelmet, and pin the three layers, together, with right sides facing.

3 Draw around the template onto the pelmet piece with a pencil.

1 Decide on the dimensions of the pelmet. Allow an extra 2in at the top to fix to the batten. Make a template for the edge using the plates.

4 Pin the fabric just inside the scalloped outline.

6 Baste along the edge, then machine-stitch with matching thread.

8 Turn the pelmet right side out and press the scalloped edge.

5 Cut out the scallops about ½in from the outline.

7 Trim the interfacing, and clip the seam allowance, so that the curves will lie flat when turned right side out.

9 Turn under the straight edge of the pelmet, then pin and machine-stitch.

10 Measure the scalloped edge and cut a length of rope to fit. Experiment with design options for the rope; for example, you could use two different colors and weights of rope.

11 Pin the rope to the pelmet and hand-stitch it in place. Attach the pelmet to the wall by using a slim batten of wood; or use Velcro to make the pelmet easy to remove.

Above: Neutral colors give the gentle shape of the pelmet a chance to make an understated impact.

Opposite: The natural linen curtains echo the pelmet fabric and are lined in a slightly darker linen, so they even look beautiful when turned back on themselves.

SHELL TIE-BACK

Curtain tie-backs can be made in a tremendously wide range of styles so you can use them to create whatever decorative effect you like. Though we normally think of a simple braid or tassel, tie-backs can be trimmed to make them focal points within the room. Here a fishing net was festooned with different types and sizes of shells. You could wire a mass of very small shells to the net or edge the curtain with a widely spaced line of shells.

YOU WILL NEED

- ♦ fishing net
- ♦ shells
- ♦ fine wire
- ♦ wire cutters
- ♦ glue gun and glue sticks or electric drill, with very fine drill bit
- ♦ string (optional)

1 Take the fishing net and arrange it in graceful folds. Gather together a mass of shells and see how they look best when arranged on the net. Cut lengths of fine wire. These can be glued to the back of the shells so that they can be wired to the netting.

2 Alternatively, drill holes in the shells. Thread string through the holes for attaching to the net.

3 Attach the shells to the netting. Make another tie-back in the same way Loop the tie-backs around the curtains and onto the wall.

CRYSTAL TIE-BACK

Mix an exquisite striped silk with crystal drops for an elegant tie-back. The trim made from a very rough burlap, bound quite casually and loosely, makes this interesting and unusual. The crystal drops were bought from an antique shop; search around for interesting examples. Failing that, use crystal drops from a bead shop or colored stones from a cheap necklace or earrings, all of which will look equally lovely.

YOU WILL NEED

♦ 1 burlap tassel tie-back

♦ scissors

♦ crystal chandelier drops

♦ gold beading wire or very fine gold string

♦ wire cutters

1 You need only one tassel tie-back for two curtains. Split the tassel in half, then unravel the rope. Rebind the tassel to make it look less formal.

2 Thread the crystal drops onto gold wire or fine string to make several lengths of various sizes.

3 Fasten the lengths of crystal drops onto the tie-backs. Some will simply hook on; others should be wired. Loop the tie-backs around the curtains and onto the wall.

SHEER MAGIC

Trim a plain linen or burlap bed cover and pillowcase with the sheerest of voile fabrics, for a look that is simple, tailored and very elegant. Large bone buttons and the rougher textures of burlap and linen are the perfect foil to the fineness of the fabric. Cut the voile a tiny bit longer than the drop on the bed so it falls gently to the floor all the way around. The voile cover is cut in three pieces, so it is easily removed and can be washed and dried within a matter of hours. The amount of voile fabric given here is for a double bed, but the basic idea can be adapted to suit any size bed.

YOU WILL NEED

- ♦ tape measure
- ♦ about 7 yd cotton voile
- ♦ dressmaker's scissors
- ♦ dressmaker's pins
- ♦ needle and basting thread
- ♦ sewing machine
- ♦ matching sewing thread
- ♦ burlap or fine linen bed cover
- ♦ 16 large bone buttons
- ♦ fine embroidery scissors
- ♦ tapestry needle
- ♦ fine string
- ♦ pillow
- ♦ burlap or fine linen

1 For the top of the cover, you will need a piece of voile the length of the bed plus the drop on one end. The piece should be 6 in narrower than the width of the bed, so the buttons will not be too near the edge. Allow 4 in all around for double hems. For the sides, you will need two pieces the length of the bed. Measure the drop from the buttons to the floor, allowing for hems.

2 Pin, baste and sew all the hems.

3 Mark the positions of the buttons and buttonholes so they correspond exactly. Sew the buttonholes and cut the centers carefully.

4 Use a tapestry needle to thread fine string through the buttons. Tie the string in a knot. Sew the buttons in position on the burlap bed cover, and button the voile cover on top.

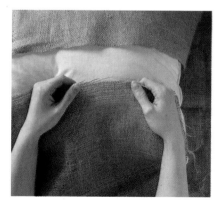

5 For the pillowcase, cut a piece of burlap the depth of the pillow and twice the length, plus seam allowances on the long sides.

6 With right sides together, pin, baste and sew the top and bottom edges. Turn right side out and press.

7 To make a fringed edge, find a thread running across the pillow, just in from the cut edge. Pull gently to fray the edge.

8 Use the same method to make an over-cover for the pillow from voile. Hem all the edges.

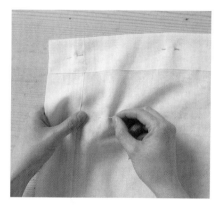

9 Mark the position of the button-holes in each corner. Machine-stitch the buttonholes and cut the centers.

10 Sew buttons to the corners of the burlap pillow cover, and button the voile cover over the top.

Right: This all-white scheme is practical as well as beautiful – the voile covers are simply unbuttoned from the main covers when they require cleaning.

PURE PLASTIC

A plastic tablecloth is invaluable on a table that gets a lot of use, as it can be wiped clean in seconds. To make it attractive as well as practical, why not cut a shaped trim and make a design along the edge using a hole punch?

1 Measure your table and cut the plastic fabric to the required size. Draw up and cut out a cardboard template or trace the template from the back of the book for the scalloped edge. Draw around the template on the wrong side of the plastic fabric.

YOU WILL NEED

♦ tape measure

♦ plastic fabric

♦ dressmaker's scissors

♦ pencil

♦ cardboard

♦ scissors

♦ hole punch

♦ ribbon, string or rope (optional)

2 Cut the edging shape with sharp dressmaker's scissors.

3 Punch out a design with a hole punch. You could thread ribbon, string or rope through the holes, to add even more interest.

TACTILE TABLECLOTH

A mass of trimmings is now available and a trip around the notions department will, with a little imagination, generate any number of ideas. Here, simple upholsterer's webbing was used to edge a burlap cloth. The webbing was decorated with string in very loose loops.

YOU WILL NEED

- about 2 yd burlap
- dressmaker's scissors
- dressmaker's pins
- needle and basting thread
- iron
- sewing machine
- matching sewing thread
- 8¾ yd webbing
- brown string

1 Cut the burlap to the size of the tablecloth you require, allowing for hems. Turn under the hems and pin, baste, press and machine-stitch. Cut a length of webbing to go around all four sides. Pin and machine-stitch the webbing around the edge.

2 Lay the string on the webbing and twist to experiment with different designs.

3 Pin, baste and hand-stitch the string to the webbing, to hold it securely. It doesn't matter if there are gaps in the stitching; the looseness of the string is all part of the effect.

ON THE SHELF

Everyone has shelves somewhere about the home, but how many of us have thought of dressing them with different styles of edging? This project includes three different designs using natural materials that would be suitable for a kitchen. Many other ideas, such as colorful fabrics, scalloped edging, ribbons, shells, buttons and bows, would be much better suited to bedrooms and bathrooms. Experiment with anything and everything around the home and you'll be surprised at just how innovative and exciting shelf edging can be. If you fix your trimmings with double-sided tape, they can be removed in an instant, so you can change the designs as often as you like.

YOU WILL NEED

- ♦ tape measure
- ♦ string
- ♦ scissors
- ♦ adhesive tape
- ♦ red raffia
- ♦ Chinese-language newspaper
- ♦ pencil
- ♦ double-sided tape or drawing pins

1 Measure the length of your shelf.

2 Cut a piece of string about 2 in longer than the shelf, so it can turn around the corners.

3 Cut more lengths of string, approximately 6–8 in long.

4 Gather together bunches of about three lengths of string.

5 Fold the bunches into loops and then pass the ends over the string and through the center of the loop. Pull the loops taut to secure them. You can tape the string to the work surface if it makes it easier to work on it.

6 Cut small pieces of red raffia and tie them into small knots between every two or three strands of looped string. Cut the raffia close to the knot.

7 For the newspaper edging, measure the shelf. Cut strips the length of the shelf, and the depth you require. Fold each strip, concertina-fashion.

8 Experiment by drawing different designs onto each folded strip.

9 Cut out the edging shapes. Open them out and smooth them flat.

10 For the raffia edging, cut a piece of raffia the length of the shelf. Cut many short lengths of raffia.

12 Tighten the loops, and fill in any gaps with more loops.

14 Use double-sided tape or drawing pins to attach the trimmings to the edge of each shelf.

11 Using one strand at a time, loop them onto the main piece, as with the string edging.

13 Trim all the ends to one length to make an even fringe.

Opposite: Shelf edging gives scope for tremendous creativity. Here, homemade fringes of raffia and string and a decorative edge cut from a Chinese-language newspaper soften wood kitchen shelves.

IN THE ROUND

Choose the primary colors of blue and red

and team them with white for a crisp,

clean look with a slightly nautical feel.

Felt is a lovely way to trim plain fabrics,

whether on shoe bags, linen bags, throws

or cushions.

YOU WILL NEED

- ♦ round template
- ♦ 2 squares red felt, about 8 x 8in
- ♦ 2 squares blue felt, about 8 x 8in
- ♦ dressmaker's pins
- ♦ fabric marker
- ♦ pinking shears
- ♦ blue cord
- ♦ string
- ♦ needle and matching sewing thread
- ♦ fabric item such as a shoebag or quilt

1 Find a template – a can lid, coin or anything round. Place the template on the felt, and draw around the template with a fabric marker. Cut around the circle with pinking shears.

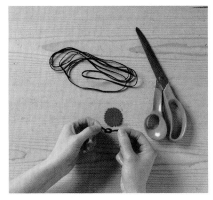

2 Pin two circles together, knot short lengths of cord and sew them to the circles.

3 Repeat with lengths of string. Sew the circles onto your shoe bag, quilt or other items.

DRESSING FOR DINNER

For very special occasions, why not take a tip from etiquette books, and give it a new twist, by preparing corsages for your chairs? Choose a style of dressing suited to the style of your furniture. Simple country chairs call for understated trimmings, whereas a fancy French one requires something much more ornate.

YOU WILL NEED

♦ silk or fresh flowers

♦ fresh greenery

♦ florist's wire

♦ scissors

♦ 2 yd organza ribbon

1 Gather your flowers and greenery. Using florist's wire, begin to wire together the stems. Using silk flowers makes life easier, because they bend to whatever shape you require.

2 Continue binding in flowers and greenery, to make an attractive corsage. Trim the stems and tuck in any ends.

3 When you're satisfied with the shape, finish with a ribbon bow. Make a wire hook to attach the corsage to the chair. If you like, make an arrangement that can be taken from the chair and worn or taken home at the end of the evening.

PRETTY POTS

Miniature topiary looks charming on a windowsill, but don't forget to make the most of their containers. Terra-cotta pots can be treated to a variety of embellishments, from tassels to tape.

YOU WILL NEED

- ♦ florist's dry foam block
- ♦ sharp knife
- ♦ 3 old terra-cotta pots
- ♦ 2 straight twigs
- ♦ glue gun and glue sticks
- ♦ 2 florist's dry foam balls
- ♦ fresh foliage such as box or privet
- ♦ selection of pebbles
- ♦ curtain weight
- ♦ fine string
- ♦ string tassels
- ♦ masking tape
- ♦ craft knife
- ♦ self-healing cutting mat
- ♦ matt varnish
- ♦ paintbrush

1 Cut the foam blocks in half and cut each block to fit into the pots. Position the foam in the pots. Insert the twigs and glue them in place, to act as the stems of the trees. Glue the foam balls on top.

2 Cut small pieces of foliage and insert them in the ball.

3 Cover the foam in the pots with a layer of small pebbles.

4 Thread the curtain weight onto string and tie it around one of the pots. Decorate the other pots with tassels, or designs cut from masking tape with a craft knife. Varnish to make the masking tape secure.

MATERIALS

You can use just about any material that catches your eye for trimmings. Although notions and interiors shops were always the traditional suppliers of trimmings such as tassels and ribbons, look beyond the expected sources for rich pickings. For natural materials in neutral colors, you could visit boating supply stores for lengths of rope in different thicknesses and textures. Try garden centers for twine and raffia and art supply stores for canvas and burlap. Take a detour from Main Street and comb the beach for interesting shells, driftwood and pebbles.

If you are looking for glamour and sparkle, bead shops have a wonderful cache of diamanté, artificial "jewels" and plastic bone to dress up glasses, napkins, tabletops and boxes.

Ribbons play such a big part in trimming, that it is worth searching out the most unusual ones possible.

Closer to home, your local post office will supply humble items such as twine, corrugated cardboard and plain brown paper – which sound unappealing but can be used to liven up anything from boxes to headboards.

The only rule in using materials for trimming is to open your eyes, collect what appeals to you and let your imagination take over.

Right: Trimming materials might include natural materials such as stones, leaves and dried materials (1); textured fabrics such as burlap (2); tassels made of cord, ribbon or raffia (3); organza ribbon (4); strings of beads or necklaces (5); shells and starfish (6); fabric paint (7); apple twigs (8); loose beads (9); string (10); and corrugated cardboard (11).

TECHNIQUES

Embellishing is all about adding — gluing, tying or sewing — basically adding to existing objects to make the simple, sensational. Part of the joy of decorating in this way is that there are no specific, professional techniques to learn, just some handy shortcuts that will make the job easier. Some quick and easy fixing techniques have been suggested here. Tassels will add glamour to any object, and although they are available in stores, they can be made at home using the materials of your choice – from silk embroidery thread to fine wire. Even the most basic of embroidery stitches will perk up plain fabric items such as napkins or pillowcases. You may not feel you have the expertise to produce intricate hand embroidery, but use thick threads in bold colors to produce large, eye-catching stitches to make your own style statement.

Blanket stitch

Fasten the working thread securely just under the fabric edge, then insert the needle down into the fabric, at the desired distance from the edge. The needle should always be at right angles to the edge, or the stitches will become uneven. Hold the working thread under the needle and pull the point of the needle through.

Buttonhole stitch

Back stitch

Bring the needle and thread up to the top side of the fabric. Reinsert the needle about ⅛in behind the point where the thread came out. Now bring the needle back up to the top, ⅛ in to the front of the first point. Continue in this way, to produce what appears to be one continuous line of stitches.

This is worked in the opposite direction of the blanket stitch. Pull the needle up through the fabric. Twist the working thread around the point of the needle. Pull the needle through the fabric, bringing the knot that has formed to the raw edge.

Using a glue gun

Hot glue will allow you to take short-cuts to fixing objects. Here, short ends of wire were glued to shells, to allow them to be tied to curtain rails, or twisted onto lengths of muslin. Always follow the manufacturer's instructions for your particular model of glue gun. Once the gun has heated sufficiently the glue becomes liquid. Be very careful; the hot glue can burn your skin. Place a small dot of glue on the surface of the object, then hold the wire on the hot glue for a few seconds until it sets completely.

Drilling holes

An alternative way of fixing objects like shells or driftwood is to drill a small hole into each, then thread a length of wire, raffia or string through the hole. For this you will need the finest drill bit available. To keep the drill from sliding off the surface, place a piece of masking tape over the spot you wish to drill, then bore the hole. Remove the masking tape and thread your chosen material through the drilled hole.

Attaching eyelets

Eyelet holes are an effective way of adding impact to plain fabrics for curtains or even bedcovers. If you are using a fairly fine fabric, you may wish to add extra body by adding interfacing to the hem. Iron-on interfacing is very easy to use. Cut the interfacing to half the depth of the hem, minus the seam allowance, and iron in place. Mark the positions of the eyelets at equal distances along the top of the curtain. Follow the manufacturer's instructions for punching the hole, then place the eyelets in position and hammer to secure. Remember to work on a very solid surface – one hard blow with the hammer should secure each eyelet.

Making tassels

1 Take 3–4 long strands of raffia. Hold together firmly, then wind them back and forth in a lazy S shape to form a skein.

2 Trim the ragged excess on the ends of the raffia.

3 Use another piece of raffia to bind tightly around the center of the skein. Tie in a firm knot (the centerpoint of the tassel), leaving two long ends that will later form the tie of the tassel. Fold the skein in half, where it has been secured, then wrap another length of raffia around it, about ⅛in from the top, to form the tassel shape. Trim the looped ends to the same length.

4 Split the two center raffia lengths to form three (raffia splits very easily). Braid to form a neat tie for the tassel, then knot when the correct length is achieved.

5 To add more body, take a pin or needle and run it down each raffia strand two or three times, to split each strand of raffia.

TEMPLATES

scalloped edge

ACKNOWLEDGMENTS

The Hop Shop
(Jacket: dried leaves on lampshade)

Josephine Ryan Antiques
(armchair, painter's desk, folding
table, plaster shapes, white jug,
candlestick, clock face and wooden
horse, page 65; glass bottles without
stoppers, page 28)

299 Antiques
(chair, pages 72–73)

*The author and publishers would like to
thank the following for the loan of
materials for photography:*

Damask Furnishings and Finery
(fine voile napkins, page 28)

Harley Antiques
(table, page 21; map box, pages 38–9)

*The author would like to thank Charles
Shirvell for his help and creative input, and
Josh George for his assistance in the studio.*

INDEX